by **Frank J. Moore**

DOVER PUBLICATIONS, INC. • NEW YORK

Instructions

Here are 28 incredible pictures that you can bring to life simply by using the specially ruled acetate screen that you'll find in the pocket at the front of the book. To make the pictures move, take the acetate screen from its pocket and lay it down flat on the picture area in the center of each page. The star on the screen should be toward the top of the page. Keeping it flat against the picture, move the screen up and down very slowly. Observe how parts of the picture actually appear to move and vibrate with life. In many cases, wiggling or tilting the screen while moving it up and down will create additional interesting patterns and effects.

Copyright © 1987 by Dover Publications, Inc.
All rights reserved under Pan American and International Copyright Conventions.

Published in Canada by General Publishing Company, Ltd., 30 Lesmill Road, Don Mills, Toronto, Ontario.
Published in the United Kingdom by Constable and Company, Ltd..

The Incredible Moving Picture Book is a new work, first published by Dover Publications, Inc., in 1987.

Manufactured in the United States of America
Dover Publications, Inc., 31 East 2nd Street, Mineola, N.Y. 11501

Library of Congress Cataloging-in-Publication Data

Moore, Frank J.
  The incredible moving picture book.

  Summary: By moving an acetate screen over the illustrations, the images which include a volcano and a sawmill appear to move and come to life.
  1. Toy and movable books—Specimens. [1. Toy and movable books. 2. Picture books] I. Title.
PZ7.M78364In 1987   [E]   87-5222
ISBN 0-486-25374-0 (pbk.)

The Waterfall

Notice that as the water plummets into the pool below, a fine spray permeates the entire area.

Ship Afire

Heavy smoke streams from the burning ship, and the sea, of course, is in constant motion.

The Deep-Sea Diver

Here at the bottom of the sea, the water appears to come to life as it ripples past an undersea explorer.

The Volcano

Thick clouds of smoke and ash are sent skyward
by this erupting volcano.

Arctic Sunset

The vibrant rays of the setting sun bring this glacial setting to life.

The Waterspout

Here the air and water have been set in turbulent motion by a twister at sea.

Boat in Distress

Caught in a disastrous storm, the small boat is pounded and nearly capsized by the crashing waves.

The Lightbulb

Observe the waves of light that appear to travel within this illuminated bulb.

The Dredge

In addition to the rippling effect of the water, notice that the spindle on this old-fashioned dredge rotates as silt is brought up from the harbor floor.

The Swimming Machine

The water rushes by as this fellow propels himself with a very ingenious device.

The Train-Track Tricycle

Watch the wheels of this most interesting vehicle turn as they traverse the rails.

The Balloonist's Misfortune

The high winds and choppy seas are not making this dramatic rescue any easier.

The Volcanic Eruption

Here you can see smoking cinder fragments from the erupting volcano plunge into the rippling water.

The Hurricane

The wind, in all its destructive glory, can be seen
here ripping apart this homestead.

The Forest Fire

Notice the motional qualities of the heat and smoke rising from the flames, as everyone who is able to flees the fire's approach.

The Tornado

This scene is visibly charged with energy as tremendous lightning bolts and a huge tornado fill the horizon.

Coastal Waves

Observe the ceaseless motion of these waves as they break over the rocky shore.

Dawn at Sea

This glorious sunrise is even more glorious when the clouds, the sun's rays and the sea are set in motion.

Lights in the Sky

This luminous phenomenon sheds an eerie, vibrant light across the land and overcast night sky.

Celestial Bodies

The planets rotate as a comet shoots through the solar system.

The Sawmill

When this sawmill is set in motion, you will
notice that several parts of the machine,
including the huge saw blade, rotate.

The Small Printing Press

Here you can observe the motion of the belts that drive the press and of the paper that runs through it.

The Large Printing Press

Follow the path of the newsprint as it travels through the press on its way to becoming newspapers.

Machine in Motion (I)

Notice that nearly every part of this machine moves, many in different directions.

Machine in Motion (II)

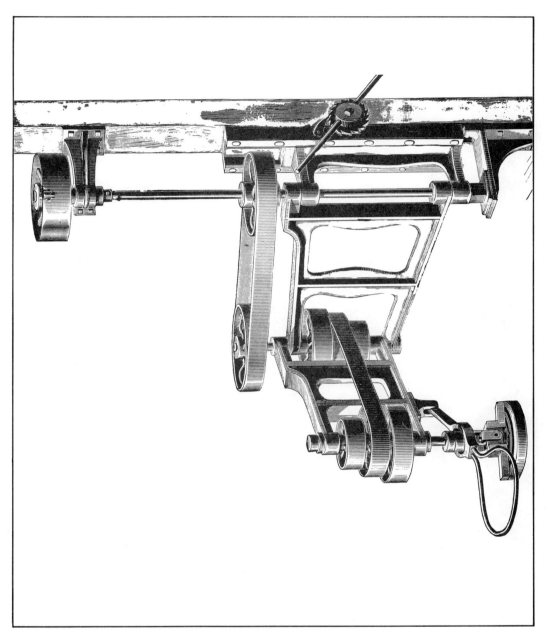

Observe the movements of the shafts, belts and other parts of this device.

Machine in Motion (III)

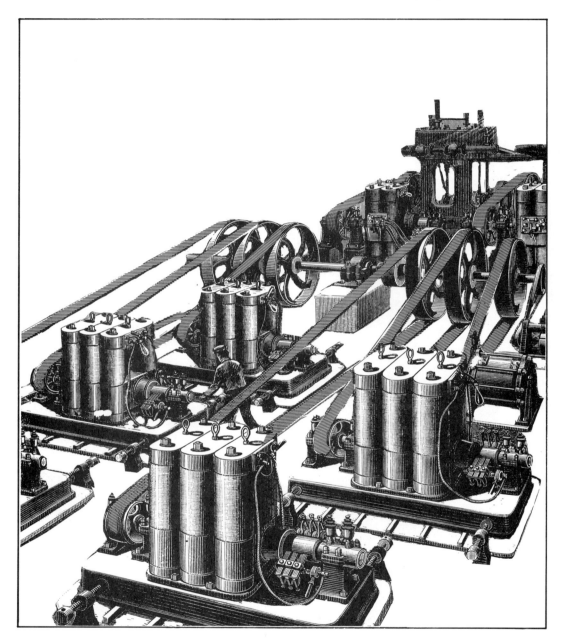

Here you'll see the large belts and shafts of this multi-engine machine in motion.

The Unusual Mill Wheel

This large mill wheel, which strangely enough looks something like a bicycle wheel, appears to be slowly turning.

The Underwater Man

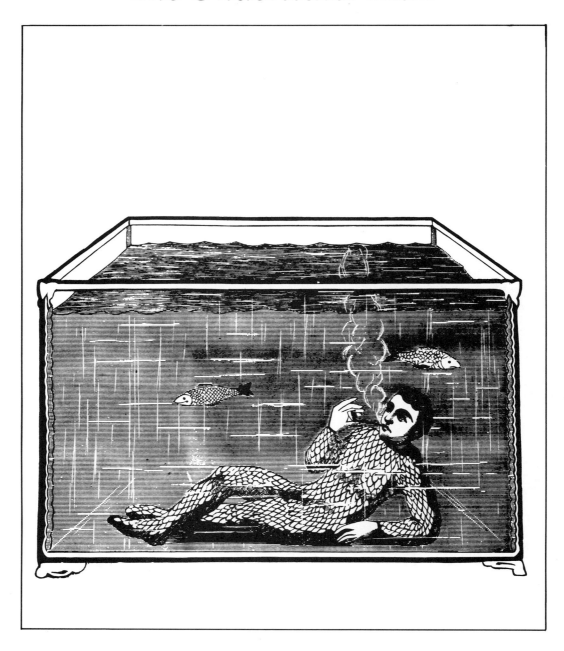

Notice how the water in this tank appears to ripple all around the two fish and their fishy companion.